THE  ESCAPE OF ALEXANDER THE GREAT

KELLY MICHELE BUCHANAN

Published by:

KMB Creative

Boynton Beach, FL

ISBN: Softcover: 978-0-69219-239-9
Hardcover: 978-0-57840-991-7

Photographs by Kelly Buchanan and Alexander

Author photo by Jessie Askinazi

Cover and interior layout by Gary A. Rosenberg
www.garyarosenberg.com

This book is affectionately dedicated to my great nephew and niece, Jacoby Everett Raymond and Elleana Jaye Raymond. I also affectionately dedicate this book to Wilfredito, Jr.

The inspiration for this book comes from my love of animals, especially my two pets: My beautiful bird, Alexander, who flew away and came back; and my ten-year-old Shihtzu, Luli.

Most important, this is a shared story about courage, true love, and a strong belief in miracles. I hope this book proves to be an inspiration to all children and their progeny.

My name is Alexander. I am an Alexandrine parrot from Sri Lanka. Before I was even old enough to fly, I was captured by traders and sold to a bird pet shop in Delray Beach, Florida.

My beginnings were humble but comfortable. There were many birds in the store beside me, from all over the world.

My cage companion and I were well fed, and we liked each other well enough. But I didn't know the first thing about love.

Then one day, a young woman came into the shop. She held me on her finger, spoke to me in her beautiful voice, and we fell in love.

That day was the start of a new life for me, and from that point on, every day was a grand adventure.

My new mom was loving and built a home for me that was like a palace.

My cage was larger than I was used to—with a large variety of food! I had seeds, pellets, fresh fruits, and veggies to eat every day, and plenty of fresh water.

My cage was very clean and had a white paper towel carpet.

Three times a week I took a bath in the stream of a spray bottle, and sometimes I even bathed in the shower!

The big day happened on a hot fall day, and the story I am going to share came to be called "The Great Escape."

I was on my perch outside my cage waiting to be sprayed. The balcony door was open, but it was covered by a shade. The wind was strong that day, and my mom left me alone to go fill the water bottle. While she was gone, the shade flapped, and I freaked.

I did what my instinct told me to do—FLY!

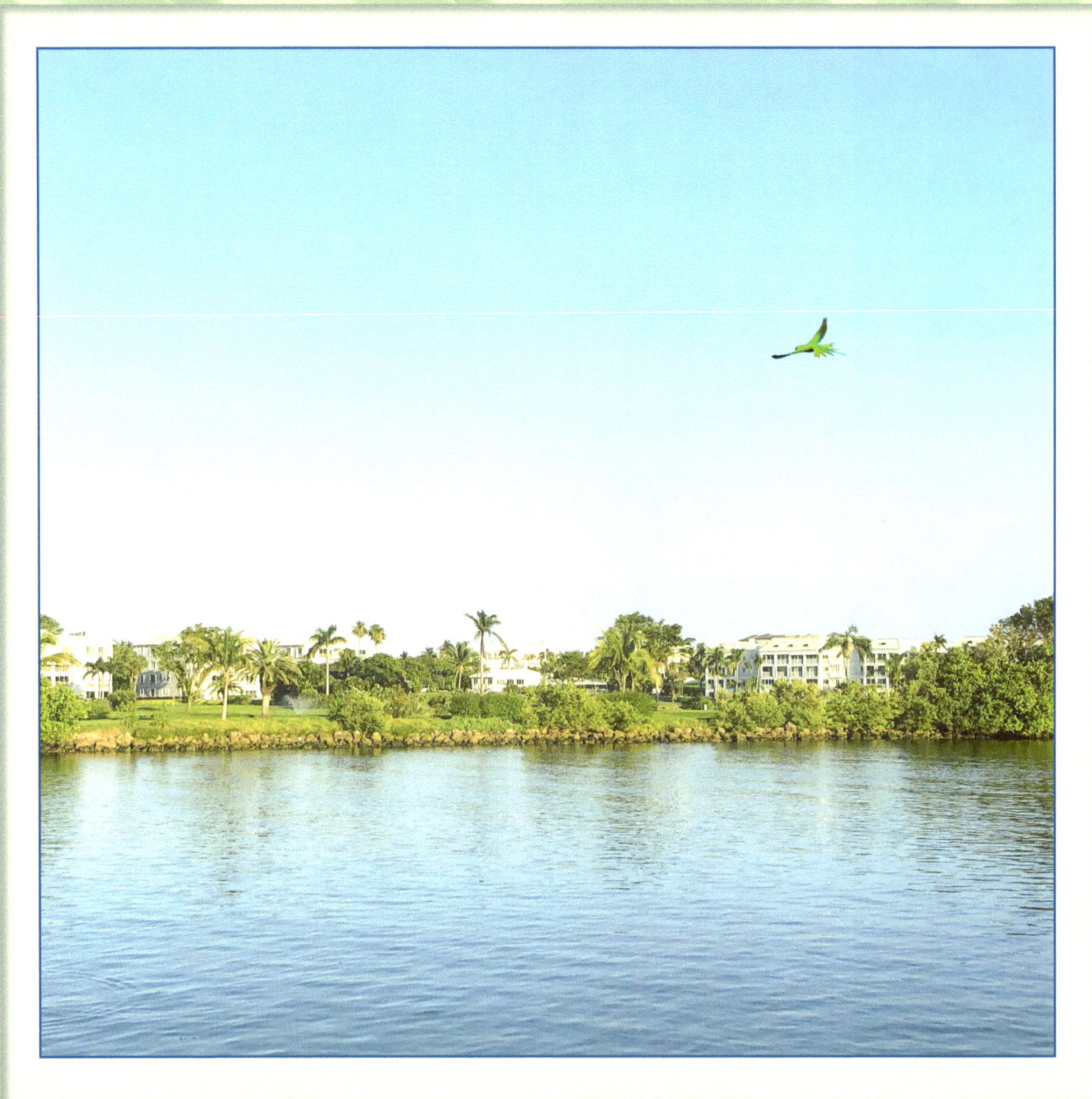

Yep, I flew out a side opening of the shade toward the east and right over Florida's Intracoastal.

It felt amazing to spread my wings. Over the water in the warm breeze I flew, taking in the sights—blue water, green palm trees, lush landscape, low buildings, and hot sun.

I was free to go anywhere, but where did I want to be? Was I really free?

Flying around was fun for a while, but as the sun began to set, I was ready to fly home.

Back over the water I flew, seeking my home. I landed in a tree by a pool and called for my mom. I called and called, and sure enough, she showed up.

She called back and frantically tried to reach me by climbing onto a chair. She couldn't reach me.

Something told me to fly, so I did—back over the water into the sunset, where I disappeared as a dot in the sky.

That night was lonely. I huddled in a tree wishing I was home. It was dark, and I was afraid to fly. Earlier, in the sky, I had seen vultures flying around searching for prey.

I am prey, I realized. I tried to sleep, but I couldn't wait for the sun to come up.

That morning, I flew back and landed in a tree in front of the building I remembered. I called and called for help, and sure enough I saw my mom.

"Alex, Alex!" she cried. "Come, Alex! Up, up..." (My mom and I were a flock, so we understood each other's language.) "You're my boy—I love you. Hi, Alex! You want yum–yum?" she asked.

I did want some yum–yum, but...

Again I had the urge to fly . . . fly into the sky, where the world shrunk below me. I flew and flew over the water, the trees, my home. Nightfall eventually came, and I found a safe spot in the trees and went to sleep.

The next day when I awoke, my mom was nowhere to be seen. I called and called, but soon I realized that I was on my own, so off I flew.

I was thirsty and hungry. I drank some dirty water from a puddle in a preserve and nibbled at some tree bark. I missed my house and my mom.

It was fun flying into freedom, but this much freedom was lonely and it took away my safety.

Flying was an experience I would never forget, but after a couple of days, I was hungry, tired, and scared. I had less and less energy to soar into the clouds, and all I wanted was to find my mom and go home.

I flew closer and closer to the ground looking for food. Finally, I landed in a bush and stayed there for a long time. I was hungry and exhausted, so when I saw two people coming closer, I thought maybe—just maybe—one of them might be my mom.

I began to call out, "C'mon, Alex. C'mon, Alex."

Neither of the people were my mom, but I kept on talking. They stopped to talk back to me, but I didn't understand them.

Soon after the people left, my mom came rushing over to the bush. I was the happiest I had ever been, and I jumped right onto her hand!

(The guard who drives the cart had seen my mom looking for me every day and night, so when the people told him they saw a beautiful bird in a bush, he told my mom right away. At least, that's what she told me.)

Soon I was back inside my home with my mom, happy to be exactly where I wanted to be.

The Escape of Alexander the Great is my story, and the moral is:

▲ Miracles can happen.

▲ Love can come at the most unexpected time.

▲ Freedom is important, but so are boundaries.

▲ We need to learn the lesson that while adventures may be exciting, they can't last forever.

An Interesting Fact

I am named after Alexander the Great. The famous Alexander the Great once had a parrot like me of his very own. He liked us so much that he named our breed after him—Alexandrine.

About the Author

Kelly Michele Buchanan, a South Florida native, believes that miracles are possible. Because of this belief, the story of *The Escape of Alexander the Great* was created.

Kelly spent her childhood surrounded by all kinds of animals. Since her parents owned a pet shop, her love of the animal world grew stronger as she got older. Kelly was inspired to share this true story about Alexander with children, since her love of animals started when she was a child.

Besides her passion of writing, Kelly has been a broker for a top Wall Street firm, a private banker, a mortgage processor, and is now a fund-raiser for a non-profit that helps small business owners.

Elleana and Kelly

Kelly still resides in South Florida with Alexander and her Shih Tzu, Luli. To keep up with the adventures of Alexander, find him at AlexBirdBook.com and on Facebook at TheEscapeofAlexandertheGreat. To stay informed on future books, visit Kelly's website at www.KellyMBCreative.com.

www.ingramcontent.com/pod-product-compliance
Lightning Source LLC
Chambersburg PA
CBHW060854270326
41934CB00002B/142